An Múchán

The Late Bronze Age Hillfort at Mooghaun South

Dr. Eoin Grogan

Director, North Munster Project

The
Discovery
Programme

© 1999 The Discovery Programme Limited.

Illustrations (unless otherwise stated) Eoin Grogan.

Design by Metaphor.

Separations by Litho Studios.

Printed by Cahill Printers.

Published by The Discovery Programme Limited.

ISBN 0-9536973-0-4

Price £4.95

Contents

Foreword

The text of this booklet is designed to provide information on the Late Bronze Age hillfort at Mooghaun South and the contemporary archaeology of the surrounding area of county Clare. It can also be used to explore the archaeology at Mooghaun and provides additional information on the interpretative panels on the site itself.

Visitors are reminded that most archaeological sites, including many of those mentioned in this text, are on private property and should only be visited with the permission of the landowner. Please respect the countryside, ensure all gates are suitably closed, and remember that you are responsible for your own safety.

The Discovery Programme

Mooghaun was investigated as part of The Discovery Programme, the archaeological research institute established by the Government in 1991. In 1992 the North Munster Project, under the Directorship of Dr. Eoin Grogan, was established to study the archaeology of this region in later prehistory, from the Middle Bronze Age to the end of the Iron Age (1600 BC to 400 AD). Excavations were carried out at Mooghaun from 1992 to 1995 as part of this research.

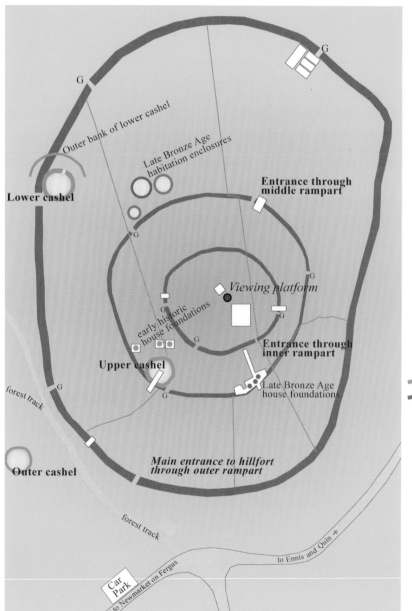

Fig. I
Site Plan.

G

Outer bank of lower cashel

Late Bronze Age
habitation enclosures

**Entrance through
middle rampart**

Lower cashel

G

G

Viewing platform

early historic
house foundations

G

G

**Entrance through
inner rampart**

Upper cashel

G

Late Bronze Age
house foundations

forest track

G

Outer cashel

*Main entrance to hillfort
through outer rampart*

forest track

☐ Excavated areas
∿ Ancient field walls (date unknown)
〰 Early historic archaeology
〰 Late Bronze Age archaeology
G Modern gap through rampart

Car
Park

to Newmarket on Fergus

to Ennis and Quin ➔

Introduction

The hillfort at Mooghaun South (Fig. 1) was built at the beginning of the Late Bronze Age, around 950 BC. At this time Mooghaun was the largest and most important site in south-east Clare. The hillfort occupies the entire hill and has commanding views over south-east Clare and the estuaries of the River Shannon (to the south) and the river Fergus (to the west).

It has three concentric lines of defence, massive walls of uncoursed stone, called *ramparts*. All three were built at the same time. The work force was drawn from a substantial part of south-east Clare. The outer rampart encloses an area of about 11 hectares (30 acres) while the inner one encloses a circular area of 0.75 hectares (1.85 acres).

Altogether the ramparts at Mooghaun consist of over 90,000 cubic metres of stone (*c.* 500,000 tonnes). It is estimated that the population of the area at the time was about 9,000 people. This could have provided a labour force of up to 3,500 that could have built the hillfort in 16 years.

Fig. 2

Map of south-east Clare showing sites and places mentioned in the text.

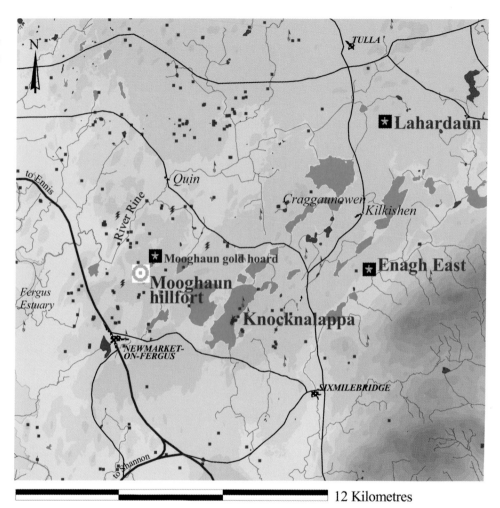

12 Kilometres

■ Towns
⋀ Main roads
⋀ Other roads
⋀ Rivers
▬ Lakes

▪ Late Bronze Age sites
★ Late Bronze Age hoards (1200–700BC)
⚡ Late Bronze Age gold artefacts
⚲ Late Bronze Age artefacts (1200–700BC)

The individual or family who directed its construction had authority over a large chiefdom. Their status was highlighted by their possession of gold ornaments, especially gorgets, collars, dress fasteners, lockrings and bracelets, as well as weapons (bronze swords, spears and knives) and tools (bronze axes, chisels, gouges and sickles). The chiefdom was sub-divided into smaller territories each controlled by an elite family.

These families lived in smaller defended hilltop sites (*e.g.* Langough, Clenagh and Cahercalla), as well as defended lakeside settlements such as Knocknalappa (Fig. 2). It is probable that these people were distinguished by their possession of weapons and tools as well as by the ornaments (gold dress fasteners and pins, bracelets and amber necklaces) that they wore.

Other important places include ceremonial enclosures. These are large sites (up to 100 metres in diameter) surrounded by a wide ditch, sometimes with an outer bank of earth. These were used for rituals that involved the whole community in each sub-territory. Some of the activities would have been associated with seasonal ceremonies intended to ensure favourable weather, the fertility of the soil, and the well-being of the people and their livestock. It appears that some ceremonies associated with the dead, possibly including part of the funerary services, were also carried out within the enclosures and fragmentary human remains have been found on several sites. Important ceremonial enclosures in the area include Coogaun, Knopoge, Rathfolan and Ballykilty (Fig. 2).

In the Late Bronze Age most burials were relatively simple cremations occasionally accompanied by coarse domestic pots. Few other grave offerings are known. Most burials were in unmarked pits although these sometimes occur in small cemeteries or are covered by mounds or barrows.

Fig. 3

View of votive offering of bronze artefacts in a lake. (National Museum of Wales).

Another significant aspect of public ritual during this part of the Bronze Age was the deposition of artefacts, mainly of gold and bronze, into wet places – lakes, bogs and rivers. The nature of these deposits shows that they were not intended to be recovered but were a form of votive offering that enhanced the status of the individuals making the deposit, as well as honouring and placating powerful spirits or deities associated with these wet places (Fig. 3).

Important hoards – collections of sacrificed metalwork – occur in this territory at Lahardaun, Enagh East (Figs 2 and 4) and Durra. The most spectacular example, containing over two hundred gold neck collars and bracelets (Fig. 5), was found on the edge of Mooghaun Lough 1km to the north of the hillfort (Fig. 2). This is the largest collection of prehistoric gold in western Europe and demonstrates the enormous power and authority of the occupants of the hillfort.[1]

Fig. 4
Photo of hoard from Enagh East.
(National Museum of Ireland).

Fig. 5
Photo of Mooghaun Hoard.
(National Museum of Ireland).

[1] Much of this spectacular hoard was melted down soon after its discovery in 1854 during the construction of the Limerick-Ennis railway. Fortunately casts were made of some of the objects and these, together with most of the surviving pieces, are on display in the National Museum of Ireland, Dublin.
Important collections of Bronze Age artefacts can be seen in the National Museum of Ireland, as well as the Limerick City Museum and the Hunt Museum, Limerick.

Social organisation in the Late Bronze Age

Mooghaun was the centre of an important and powerful territory in the Late Bronze Age. This covered an area of about 450 square kilometres and was divided into smaller territories (of about 25km²), each with its own defended hilltop settlement (such as Langough and Cahercalla), or a lakeshore settlement enclosed by a timber palisade (such as Knocknalappa)(Figs 2 & 6).

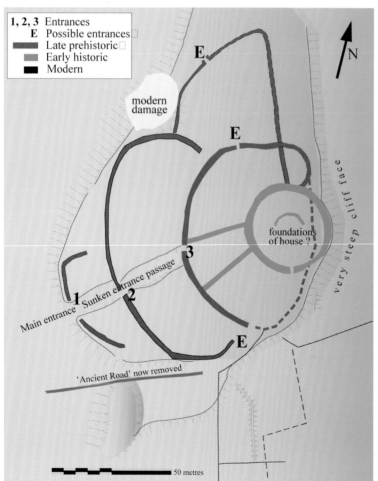

Fig. 6
Plan of hilltop enclosure at Langough (after Westropp).

The partly levelled fort at **Langough** was studied by the noted antiquarian T. J. Westropp at the end of the nineteenth century when it was still very well-preserved. It had at least three lines of defence dating to late prehistory, as well as a cashel and other walls built in the early historic period (*c*. 800 AD). It was built on a small hillock bounded on the east side by a low, steep, cliff.

Fig. 7

Map of Mooghaun area showing possible territorial organisation.

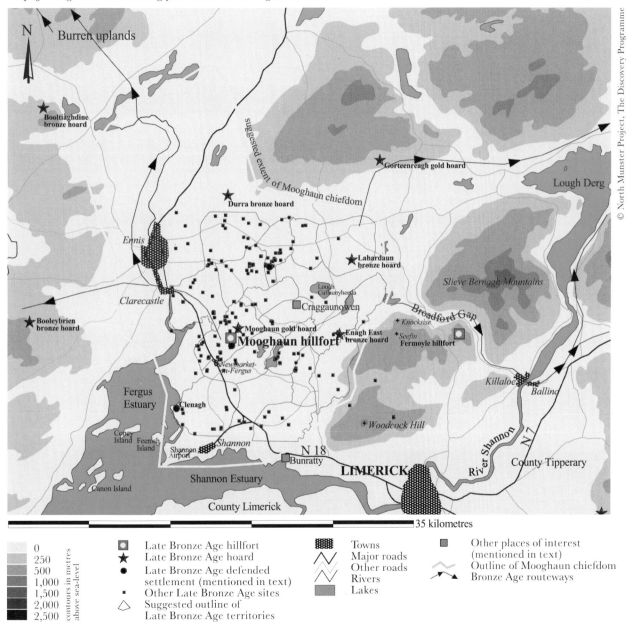

Labels on map:
Burren uplands
Booltiaghdine bronze hoard
suggested extent of Mooghaun chiefdom
Gorteenreagh gold hoard
Lough Derg
Durra bronze hoard
Ennis
Lahardaun bronze hoard
Slieve Bernagh Mountains
Clarecastle
Lough Cullaunyheeda
Craggaunowen
Broadford Gap
Booleybrien bronze hoard
Mooghaun gold hoard
Mooghaun hillfort
Enagh East bronze hoard
Knocksise
Seefin
Fermoyle hillfort
Newmarket-on-Fergus
Fergus Estuary
Clenagh
Killaloe
Ballina
Cooey Island
Feenish Island
Woodcock Hill
Canon Island
Shannon Airport
Shannon
Bunratty
N 18
LIMERICK
River Shannon
N 7
County Tipperary
Shannon Estuary
County Limerick

35 kilometres

Legend:
contours in metres above sea-level:
0
250
500
1,000
1,500
2,000
2,500

◉ Late Bronze Age hillfort
★ Late Bronze Age hoard
● Late Bronze Age defended settlement (mentioned in text)
▪ Other Late Bronze Age sites
△ Suggested outline of Late Bronze Age territories

▓ Towns
∿ Major roads
∿ Other roads
∿ Rivers
▨ Lakes

▪ Other places of interest (mentioned in text)
∿ Outline of Mooghaun chiefdom
➤ Bronze Age routeways

15

Fig. 8
Late Bronze Age sword from the River Shannon at Killaloe, Co. Clare.
(National Museum of Ireland).

The occupants of these smaller hilltop sites made up the aristocracy of the period and in addition to controlling the agricultural production of their territories would have been distinguished by their possession of weapons (Fig. 8), and of personal ornaments such as gold bracelets, dress fasteners and pins, and amber necklaces.

Smaller settlements, occupied by less important families, were enclosed by low stone banks and are generally sited on west and south facing slopes or low natural rock platforms (Fig. 11). Each appears to be the residence of an individual family and excavated examples have produced evidence for a single round house and occasional smaller farm buildings. About fifty of these habitation enclosures have been identified in the Mooghaun area (Fig. 2). These enclosures often occur in clusters, probably representing kingroups, within systems of both small and large fields. This suggests that there may have been a co-operative approach to farming. Each group appears to have farmed an area of between 154 hectares and 315 hectares and it is estimated that the population in each of these units was about 35 to 100 people. Although none has been discovered in the Mooghaun area, evidence from other parts of Ireland shows that there were also many unenclosed occupation sites, possibly representing another, lower, tier in society.

Within each unit there are also ritual sites, including standing stones and some burial mounds. The most common sites of the period are cooking places *(fulachta fiadh)* of which there are over 200 examples surviving in the territory controlled

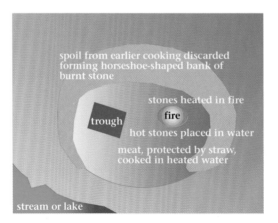

spoil from earlier cooking discarded forming horseshoe-shaped bank of burnt stone

stones heated in fire

fire

trough

hot stones placed in water

meat, protected by straw, cooked in heated water

stream or lake

Fig. 9
*Plan (left) and reconstruction drawing (right) of **fulacht fiadh**.*

from the hillfort (Figs 2 and 9). These consist of a central trough (of stone or wood) set into the ground in a wet area (such as the edge of a lake) which fills naturally with water; this was heated by placing heated stones into it and the boiling water was used to cook meat wrapped in straw.[1]

The shattered stones cleared from the trough before the next use were piled around the trough in a horseshoe-shaped mound (leaving access from one side to the trough) giving these sites their characteristic shape. Research has shown that in this area most cooking places could only be used in high summer; some of them were re-used on more than 350 occasions. The location of these sites, within the ambit of the settlement clusters but set apart from the habitation sites in marginal wet ground, suggests that they were used as feasting sites by the kingroups on a seasonal basis. While these feasts were essentially an opportunity for socialising and family bonding it is possible that other local ceremonies and rituals were associated with these special occasions.

[1] A working example of a *fulachta fiadh* can be seen in the Heritage Park at Craggaunowen.

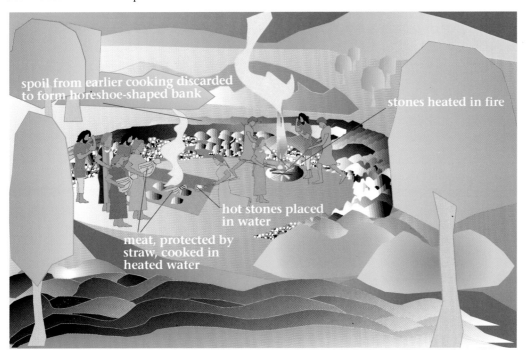

spoil from earlier cooking discarded to form horeshoe-shaped bank

stones heated in fire

hot stones placed in water

meat, protected by straw, cooked in heated water

The role of the hillfort

Mooghaun was the central site in a complex social, political and economic network that dominated south-east Clare from *c.* 1000 to 750 BC. It appears to have been built as a political statement at the beginning of the Late Bronze Age at a time when momentous changes were taking place in the nature of social and political power. A new elite who wielded power over the whole sub-region emerged and the construction of the hillfort appears to have been a marker in the development of their authority. We should envisage this new political unit (or chiefdom) as being made up of several communities who were themselves involved in its creation. They were able to identify with the new social order and the increased sense of place (belonging to and identifying with a particular area) that emerged. The suggestion is that the people within the Mooghaun chiefdom had a real sense of belonging to it, to the area it controlled and to the special place of Mooghaun as the symbol of their identity. So Mooghaun is a monumental emblem to a new order. We can parallel this development of new political authorities elsewhere in the country at this time and neighbouring chiefdoms seem to have been established around Fermoyle in east Clare (Fig. 2), and on the Burren in north Clare, perhaps centred on the hillfort at Turlough Hill. Others have been identified in counties Kerry, Limerick and Tipperary.

How the fort was built

Mooghaun occupies the whole summit of a limestone hill and comprises three ramparts that in total enclose 11.05 hectares and consist of a total length of 2.10 kilometres. The plan of the site shows that the builders attempted to maintain a regular, if not symmetric, relationship between the three ramparts and that the site was envisaged and planned as a single integrated structure. As we can imagine, its construction could only have been attempted if the whole hill was largely cleared of vegetation and if the builders had a thorough understanding of the terrain of the hill. We know from vegetation studies that Mooghaun was cleared before the fort was built and evidence from the excavation shows that scrub on the hilltop was burnt immediately before the ramparts were erected. One other design problem remained: the rocky and irregular topography of the hill itself. To overcome this the builders had to achieve a balance between the desire to retain a constant relationship between the ramparts and the desire to take maximum advantage of the defensive qualities of the hill terrain: each rampart needed to be set along the outer edge of a natural step in the limestone. The result is a remarkable achievement, one that required a very detailed knowledge of the site and considerable co-ordination of the actual building programme.

Each rampart was built, where possible, where its apparent height would be enhanced by the micro-topography (Fig. 10). This maximised the effect while minimizing the amount of work required. The position of each rampart appears to have been laid out using lines of large boulders and blocks that were adjusted until the final design was achieved. These lines, and the full rampart that later engulfed them, consist of a series of relatively straight sections linked together to give a generally polygonal, rather than totally curvilinear, plan. The construction work involved the initial erection of a stone bank defined by two lines of blocks that formed the spine of the rampart. Slabs and blocks of limestone were then stacked against the outer face to widen the ramparts and the final touch was to more carefully revet the inner face with either a low drystone wall or a line of large slabs (Figs 14 and 19). Surprisingly, there is no evidence that there was any attempt to construct a vertical outer face for the rampart. The one exception is in the area immediately around the main entrance through the outer rampart where the outer face of the inner bank had a drystone facing (Fig. 10). Although the structure of the ramparts is generally similar throughout the site there are some interesting variations in the details of construction. These seem to have been in part due to the variation in the nature of the limestone available on each area of the hill, as well as to the differing engineering solutions required depending on the terrain.

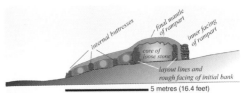

Middle rampart south side
(width 8.5 metres, 28 feet)

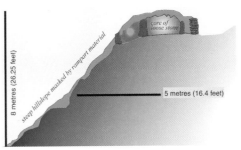

Middle rampart west side
(width 10 metres, 33 feet)

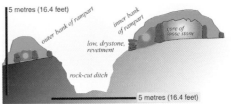

Outer rampart south side
(overall width 12.5 metres, 41 feet)

Fig. 10
Profiles across the ramparts.

The function of the hillfort

But what of the function of the hillfort? The excavation evidence shows that only a relatively small community of perhaps 10 to 12 families, the ruling elite and their retinue perhaps, lived within the fort. We can be certain that the land within the hillfort itself constituted the primary farmland of the occupants and that there would have been small tillage plots, grazing and probably managed woodland within the defences. It has long been believed that Irish hillforts were mainly places of gathering, on special occasions or at times of danger, for the people who lived in their vicinity. Certainly we can accept that Mooghaun had one such purpose and we can imagine that communal ceremony, drawing on people from the whole chiefdom, took place on the hilltop. This would have served to enhance the bonding of society as well as providing occasions where important social interaction and negotiation, trade, exchange, agreements and disputes were discussed and settled.

The site of the hillfort was chosen carefully as it is the most prominent location within the hilly lakeland terrain of south-east Clare. The fort was built here, not just to provide a commanding (and strategic) view over the chiefdom, but to be clearly visible within the area as a constant reminder of the authority of the elite and the strength and vigour of its people. This in part helps to explain the nature of the hillfort ramparts. In some areas these are very imposing defensive features; on the west side of the hill, for example, the middle rampart is set on a high natural step in the limestone hill. The builders extended the rampart down the face of the step in order to give it the appearance of an enormous constructed barrier nearly 8 metres (26.25 feet) high (Fig. 10). In other areas, for example on the south side, the middle rampart was never more than 2 metres in height. Another important factor is that in terms of fortification it is clear that even the circuit of the inner enclosure would require a large force to defend it against concerted attack, certainly one many times larger than could be drawn from the occupying community of less than one hundred people. In other words, we should not view Mooghaun as a fort in the modern sense: it was built to look impressive, both from a distance and close up, and any defended section of it provided an effective and defensible barrier against attack. As a fortification its role was largely, if monumentally, symbolic.

We can visualise just how imposing a site the new hillfort would have been, freshly cleared of trees and other scrub, with its gleaming pale-grey ramparts of fresh limestone: a breath-taking monument demonstrating the power and wealth of the new chiefdom and visible throughout south-east Clare.

"I told you there were only two of them, Ted"

The organisation of the Late Bronze Age landscape

The evidence from the Mooghaun area shows that the ordering of society was mirrored by the organisation of the landscape in which Late Bronze Age people lived (Fig. 11). At a local level families and kingroups farmed extensive areas of land. The inner areas, as within the confines of the hillfort itself (Fig 16), were divided into fields separated by stone walls, fences or hedgerows. Most of the intensive day-to-day tillage and stock raising would have been carried out in close proximity to the habitation enclosures. Beyond these would have been a less intensively ordered zone that would have included extensive tracts of managed woodland (for building materials and firewood), and probably unfenced rough grazing. Some seasonal pasture at a further remove would have occurred along the margins of the tidal estuaries of the larger rivers (the Shannon, Fergus, Rine and Owenogarney/Ratty) and in upland areas, perhaps along the fringes of the Slieve Bernagh Mountains and Cratloe Hills to the east of Mooghaun.

Fig. 11

Stylised map of landscape and social organisation in the Late Bronze Age.

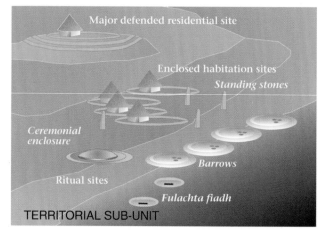

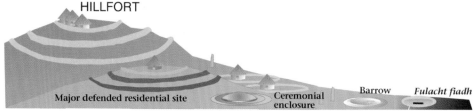

Small ritual and ceremonial monuments, such as *fulachta fiadh*, standing stones, burial sites and barrows, formed part of this local, familial, landscape. At this level we can envisage that each local community had its own identity and its own expressions of social and ceremonial occasions. Local festivities and rituals, probably including the commemoration of births, marriages, deaths, funerals and seasonal gatherings, would have enhanced both communal identity and bonding. The archaeological evidence suggests that several of these kingroups were contained within a territory controlled by elite families who resided in defended hilltop or lakeshore settlements. The integration of the population within this broader unit was maintained by the authority of this elite, but also by the social, ceremonial and historical bonds of the community. One important context for this shared sense of belonging would have been the ceremonial enclosures and the rituals and festivities held within them on special occasions during the annual cycle.

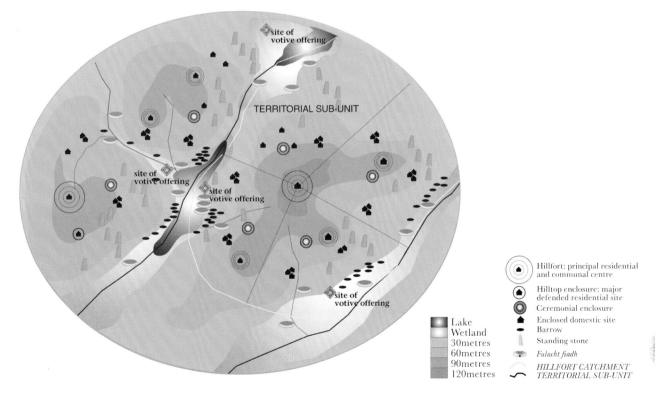

At the highest level of social and political organisation, forming also the central point for the management of the landscape, was the hillfort at Mooghaun and its chiefly family. The allegiance of the other territorial elites was probably maintained by a series of social and economic bonds and mutual obligations. These may have been expressed in elements such as marriage, gift exchange, shared ceremonial and ritual occasions, as well as in the wearing of elaborate personal ornaments and the possession of splendid weaponry. Indeed, this elite group has often been referred to as a warrior aristocracy.

This general division of society, and the organisation of the landscape, into a threefold hierarchy is one that can be compared to another aspect of Late Bronze Age behaviour, the votive deposition of metal artifacts into wet places. At the lower end of the scale there are many offerings of single objects, axes, swords, spearheads and even ornaments, which suggest the sacrifices of individuals or small communities. Above this are the hoards, such as Enagh East (Figs 2 and 4), and Lahardaun (Figs 2 and 5), that may have symbolised a territorial offering and are certainly found close to major hilltop enclosures. Other hoards in county Clare of this type have been found at Durra (Fig. 7), Teernagloghane and Booltiaghadine. The great gold hoard from Mooghaun North (Figs 2 and 5) seems to represent an event special to the whole population of the chiefdom, one that would have enhanced the status of the ruling elite but would also have reflected glory on the entire society. Other hoards of this stature may be those from Gorteenreagh, which contained the regalia of a chiefly person, and Booleybrien (Fig. 7), which contained a bronze horn probably used on great ceremonial occasions.

Photo of hoard from Booleybrien, Co. Clare.
(National Museum of Ireland).

Mooghaun South
the archaeological trail

This section follows the archaeological trail across Mooghaun and incorporates expanded versions of the Information Panels 2-10.

The Main Hillfort Entrance

This is the main entrance through the first line of defence.

The entrance passes through two massive stone walls separated by a ditch. A stout gate would have guarded this, with sentries observing anybody approaching the fort (Fig. 12).

Fig. 12
Reconstruction drawing of main hillfort entrance. (David Hill).

When the rampart was built the ditch was dug 2 metres into the underlying limestone bedrock but is now filled with debris tumbled from the stone banks. The inner bank was originally up to 1.5 metres higher than at present and the lower portion of it was faced with a drystone wall of large blocks (Fig. 13). Although the population of the hillfort would never have been large enough to defend even the inner enclosure against serious, concerted, attack the size of its defences was intended to appear impenetrable. This entrance was therefore the most important point of access to the site and would, in addition, have been the point of entry for important visitors, or ceremonial processions.

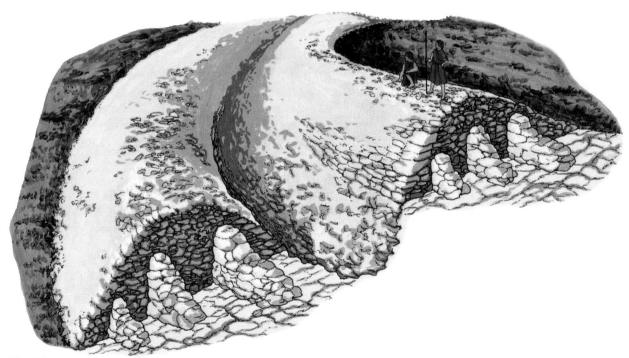

Fig. 13
Isometric section through outer rampart. (David Hill).

Information Panel 3

The Middle Rampart

The middle rampart was a stone bank, similar to that of the other two ramparts.

The bank here is poorly preserved because stone was taken from it to build the later ringfort (cashel)(Fig. 14); you can see undamaged sections immediately to the east and north-west. In this area the rampart was originally 5-7 metres wide and up to 2 metres high (Fig. 10). The gap at this point is a modern feature.

Fig. 14
Reconstruction drawing showing the middle rampart being dismantled during the construction of the early historic cashel. (David Hill).

The bank was built almost entirely of limestone from the hill itself but some sandstone, which occurs naturally on the hill as glacial debris, was also used. The limestone came from three main sources – loose stones on the surface, large irregular slabs lifted from the upper surface of the limestone rock, and stone taken from at least two large quarries on the hilltop. The stone used in each section of the ramparts reflects the source and quality of the material available in the immediate area. There is no indication that timber was used in any part of the hillfort construction.

View of the cashel wall overlying the hillfort rampart.

Excavation of the cashel in progress.

The Cashel and House Sites

This small stone fort (cashel) was built after the middle of the first millennium AD, about 1,500 years after the hillfort.

The cashel was built on top of the middle rampart of the hillfort and much of the building material was robbed from the middle and inner ramparts of the hillfort. The stone wall survives to most of its original height of about 2 metres and encloses a level area 29 metres in diameter. Excavation at other similar sites indicates that a timber gate would have protected the entrance. At this time the hilltop was re–occupied and the evidence suggests an extensive population represented by three cashels, several unenclosed round houses, a major workshop area near the hill summit (involving the working of iron, bronze and stone) and a large field system with associated animal pens.

Fig. 15

Reconstruction drawing of the cashel and its associated houses. (David Hill).

The cashel would have been occupied by an important extended family that farmed the area around the hill. There was a circular house and perhaps small farm buildings (indicated by the foundations of a structure immediately inside the fort on the right) inside the cashel (Fig. 15). These farmsteads were largely self-sufficient and a range of industrial activities, including iron, bronze, wood, leather and bone working, spinning, dyeing and weaving, and wood turning are a common feature of these sites. Domestic animals included cattle (which had a special status as the principal form of valuation), sheep, pigs, dogs and chickens, and a variety of crops including wheat, barley and rye were grown. The house sites immediately outside the cashel were probably occupied by families of lesser status tied to the working of the farmland.

This site was used as a viewing platform and possible picnic spot for the estate of Dromoland Castle in the late eighteenth or early nineteenth century. This would explain the destruction of the interior – probably as a result of tree planting and their more recent removal – as well as the numerous repairs to the wall which can be identified by the different masonry styles.

Aerial view of the cashel. House foundations outlined. (Aoife Daly).

House foundations during excavation.

Entrance through the Inner Rampart

Here the path crosses into the inner enclosure, but this does not appear to be an original entrance.

Although this was the most important area of the hillfort we do not have any precise knowledge of the activities within it other than houses and domestic settlement on the eastern side. It is probable that this was the area within which special social gatherings

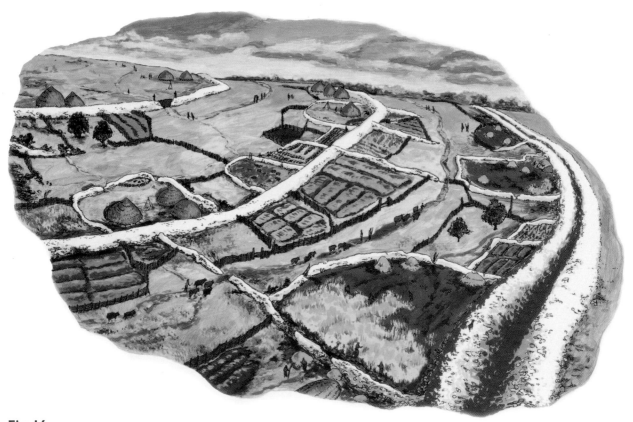

Fig. 16
View of the south-eastern side of the hillfort. (David Hill).

and ceremonies relating to the whole of the Mooghaun territory were held. The cairn, which may have been built in the Early or Middle Bronze Age up to a thousand years before the hillfort, could have acted as a symbolic focus for these gatherings.

Access to the inner enclosure was by a single entrance. This is a narrow passage that zigzags through the rampart and may have been sealed by more than one gate. The track leading to this had to meander around the hill following a circuit between the staggered entrances through the three ramparts. The main activity areas – tillage fields, houses, workshops – were along this routeway concentrating on the south-east sides of the hill (Fig. 16).

The main domestic focus was along the inner edge of the middle enclosure. Evidence from the excavations suggests that the expansive area enclosed between the outer and middle ramparts (8.2 hectares, 20.25 acres) was devoted to a mixture of tillage within small fields, unenclosed grazing and woodland management. Small pens for animals have been found dotted around this area; the rough, slightly unstable surface of the ramparts would have deterred cattle from straying outside the hillfort (and would have prevented them from being quietly driven off!) but sheep, and especially goats, would have had to be penned or tethered. Pigs, which were an important source of meat for the occupants, may have been loose within and around the woodland on the site.

Aerial view of the middle and inner ramparts, and the upper cashel, from the south-west. (Aoife Daly).

The Inner Enclosure

The Mooghaun territory was occupied by farming communities who grew cereals and raised cattle, sheep, and pigs. They also had horses and dogs.

The community here seems to have been quite wealthy. Although valuable artefacts are rarely found on settlement sites these people had a rich diet based on mixed farming of wheat, cattle and pigs. They also raised some sheep, probably for their wool, and had horses and dogs. They produced a large number of bucket-shaped pottery vessels, mainly for cooking and storage. Simple tools of bone and stone were also recovered during the excavations.

Study of the plant history of the area has shown that the first major phase of human occupation of the area coincided with the clearance of the hilltop to prepare for the building of the fort. The farmland was divided into small fields close to the settlements, but further away there were larger fields (for grazing) and open areas. Small areas of woodland were managed to provide building material and firewood.

Mooghaun appears to have been the centre of a major trade route running from the river Fergus in the west to the Broadford Gap in the north-east where it led onto the River Shannon and the important prehistoric ford at Killaloe. The control of this route-way may have added considerably to the wealth and status of the hillfort occupants. The valuable tools, weapons, and gold ornaments were probably made by highly skilled craft workers operating under the patronage of important ruling families such as those who occupied the major defended settlements (Fig. 17). It is probable that the whole process of production, including the mining of raw materials, the manufacture of the artefacts and the access to ownership of the finished objects, was controlled by these elites. These objects symbolised the authority of the elite families and their occasional sacrifice – by throwing them into lakes, rivers and bogs – added to the prestige of their owners (Fig. 3).

Fig. 17
Reconstructed scene of exchange during the Late Bronze Age. (David Hill).

The Viewing Platform

From here, the highest point of the hillfort, you get a commanding view of the surrounding countryside.

Fig. 18

Features in the landscape and on the horizon as viewed from the summit of Mooghaun hill. (David Hill).

Although much of the hilltop is now covered by trees, in the Bronze Age the area was substantially clear of vegetation and the whole of south-east Clare, as well as parts of north Limerick, would have been visible from this vantage point (Fig. 19). As important, was the fact that the hill would have been a major focal point that could be seen from throughout the area.

North West

Nearby is Mooghaun Towerhouse, then Castlefergus Towerhouse, and beyond the main Limerick-Ennis-Galway road. Clearly visible beyond are the towns of Clarecastle and Ennis, and on the horizon, the Burren Uplands.

West-south-west

In the foreground is Dromoland Woods and Castle, and beyond that the Fergus Estuary and the west Clare uplands.

South West

In the foreground is the confluence of the Shannon and Fergus Estuaries (Feenish, Coney and Canon Islands), with the knoll of Clenagh (surmounted by a hilltop enclosure), and further away, county Limerick with the Aughinish Alumina factory (chimneys) and, on the horizon, the uplands of west Limerick and Ballylin Hillfort.

South

The broad expanse of the Shannon Estuary dominates the background with beyond it the rolling lowlands of mid Limerick. Newmarket-on-Fergus (Church spire) is visible in the foreground with, beyond it, Shannon Airport a little to the west.

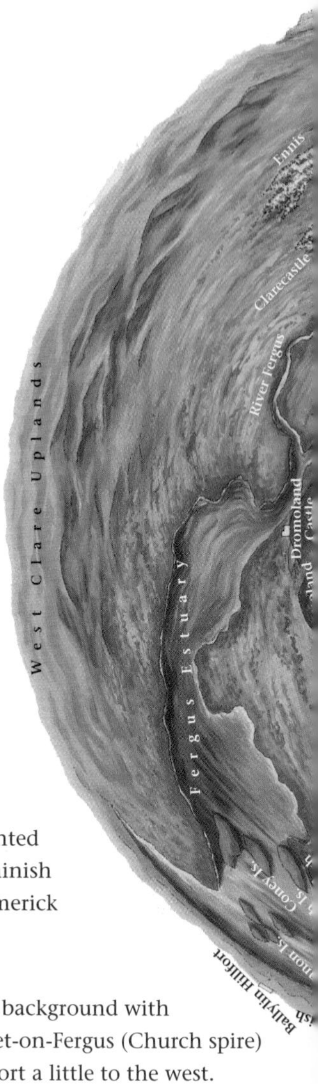

North

The town of Quin and its Cistercian abbey are in the middle foreground with the North Clare Uplands on the horizon.

North-east

In the foreground is the low hill of Caherkine. In the mid foreground are the lakes of Mooghaun (where the gold hoard was found) and Ataska, and on the horizon, Craggaunowen. The peaks of Knocksise (256 metres/840 feet) and Seefin (295 metres/968 feet) hide the Broadford Gap that leads through the mountains from east Clare to the River Shannon. The site of the hillfort at Fermoyle is visible on the horizon between Knocksise and Seefin.

East-north-east

In the foreground is the low hill of Caherscooby, beyond which is the area of lakelands around the town of Kilkishen, and on the horizon, the Slieve Bernagh mountains.

East

In the foreground is the hilly lakeland terrain around the town of Kilmurry, with the complex at Enagh East in the further distance and the summit of Knockaphunta (309 metres/1,014 feet) on the horizon.

East-south-east

In the mid foreground are Rosroe Lough and Finn Lough, the Late Bronze Age lakeshore settlement at Knocknalappa, and towards the horizon the peaks of Fisherman's Hill and Gallowshill.

South-east

Beyond the edges of Finn and Rosroe Loughs is the southern peak of the Cratloe Hills (Woodcock Hill, 310 metres/1,017 feet) with the chimneys of the cement factory at Limerick on the horizon.

South-south-east

Beyond the lowlands of south Clare is Bunratty Castle on the shore of the Shannon Estuary with, in the distance, Carrigogunnel Castle in county Limerick.

Map labels: Burren, North Clare Uplands, Broadford Gap, Craggaunowen Castle, Craggaunowen, Knocksise, Fermoyle Hillfort, Seefin, River Rine, Quin Abbey, Knappogue Castle, Caherkine Fort, Mooghaun Towerhouse, Mooghaun Lough, Lough Ataska, Finn Lough, Rosroe Lough, Knocknalappa, Shannbridge, Newmarket on Fergus, Lough Gash, Fisherman's Hill, Gallowshill, Cratloe Hills, Limerick, River Owengarney, Bunratty Castle, Shannon Town, Carrigogunnel Castle, Shannon Estuary, Airport

Leaving the Inner Enclosure

At this point we leave the inner enclosure of the hillfort through a break in the rampart wall.

Fig. 19

Isometric section through the inner rampart showing the sequence of construction. (David Hill).

Here we can see an excavated section through the middle rampart that shows the way that the defences were built (Fig. 19). The first task of the hillfort builders was to decide on the position of each of the three ramparts and the line that each would follow. This was marked by two lines of large blocks or boulders (1) that were then built up to a height of about 1 metre. The space between these was then filled with a core of loose stone and limestone rubble (2). The next step was to stack material against the outer face of the rampart (3) to buttress the core. Finally, a more carefully built inner face, of stacked blocks or upright slabs (4) was erected.

View of the excavation of the inner rampart showing details of construction. (Tom Condit).

Information Point

Leaving the Middle Enclosure

At this point we leave the inner enclosure of the hillfort through a break in the rampart wall. This location is marked **(i)** *on the site plan (back cover flap).*

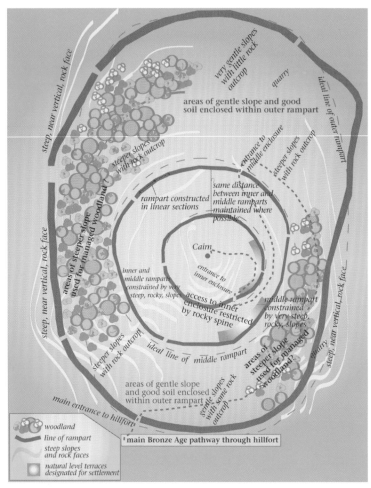

Fig. 20

Drawing showing the layout and construction of the ramparts.

This is one of the best-preserved portions of the hillfort defences. It consists of a very substantial bank of stones 10 metres wide and standing over 2 metres high. Beyond the rampart to the right (north-east) are the foundations of three smaller enclosures (12–25 metres in diameter). These probably date to the Middle Bronze Age (*c.* 1200BC) and were occupied by individual families of relatively low status. They were abandoned when the hillfort was built and the stone from them was used in the middle rampart.

As mentioned earlier the hillfort represents a massive undertaking by the population of the Mooghaun chiefdom. The estimated population of the territory (9,000 people) could have provided a work-force of 3,000 to 3,500 on an annual, seasonal basis. If such a group worked for three months of the year the hillfort could have been built in 16 years. We don't know how such a labour force was organised but we believe it was motivated by two factors: the authority of the ruling family and the wish to build something in which the whole of the participating community could identify and take pride. The actual construction of the ramparts provides some insight into how the work was undertaken. None of the ramparts follow smooth curvilinear lines; they consist instead of straight lengths of wall 30–100 metres long that have marked junctions with the adjoining sections (Fig. 20). Each section, while following a general building design, varies slightly from the others in the detail of its construction. This suggests that a different group built each section: could it be that each community within the Mooghaun chiefdom was allocated, under overall supervision, the building of a particular portion of the hillfort? This may have introduced an element of productive rivalry while also increasing the communities' commitment to the project.

Material for the ramparts consists of loose stone scattered across the hillside, the surface stone of the limestone bedrock (prised loose using fire-hardened wooden wedges and levers, and stone hammers) and rock quarried from the steep rock faces on the eastern and western sides of the hill. Leather sacks and woven baskets were probably used to transport the smaller stones with wooden pallets used for the larger blocks of stone.

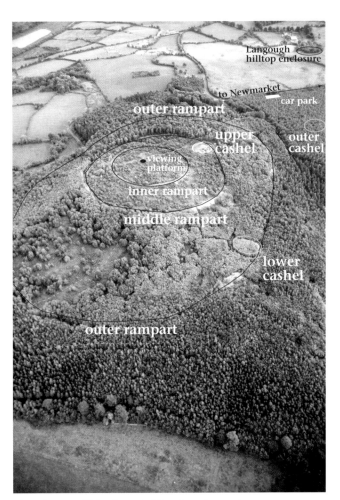

Aerial view of Mooghaun hillfort from the north. (Aoife Daly).

Bronze Age House Sites

These house sites, between the inner and middle ramparts, were built at the time of the occupation of the hillfort.

The most intensive Late Bronze Age settlement within the hillfort occurred along this gentle south-facing slope below the summit of the hill (Fig. 16). These house sites would have been occupied by people who were closely connected to the ruling family. They may have belonged to craftsmen, farmers or warriors. They had a very high proportion of pork in their diet which at this time was an indication of high status.

Although much of the evidence in this area of the fort was damaged by nineteenth century agriculture, it appears that the population of the hillfort consisted at most of about ten families (Fig. 22). Each occupied a round house with an interior 5 metres in diameter. The houses were used mainly for sleeping, cooking, perhaps some craft activities such as weaving, and socialising in the evenings; so a floor area of 20 square metres was ample for a family of five to seven people (Fig. 21). The houses probably had conical thatched roofs and a central hearth. Both beaten earth floors and internal paving have been found in the houses. These were sturdy, warm buildings and there is evidence for much repaired paved areas between them to keep the domestic area mud free.

Fig. 21
Reconstruction drawing of a Late Bronze Age house. (David Hill).

While life in the Bronze Age was far from primitive it could be harsh and this is shown in the evidence of both physical condition and life expectancy derived from the burial evidence. Although the people had a varied, nutritious diet there is some indication of periodic food shortage reflecting an incidence of animal disease and crop failure in an era before modern drugs and sprays. This is partly reflected in the average height of the

Fig. 22

Reconstruction of main Late Bronze Age settlement area. (David Hill).

population. Human disease must also have been prevalent and the very high infant mortality is also a factor in the surprisingly low life expectancy figures of 32 years for men and 28 years for women; the latter reflects the particular dangers to both mothers and infants at and following birth. Nevertheless, having survived the first more precarious years of life many individuals lived well into their fifties and enjoyed robust health. This is shown by the quality of bone healing after breakage (which also indicates the high level of basic health care) and by the condition of most skeletal material. One feature of the period is the very high incidence of arthritis, even amongst teenagers and young adults.

The Lower Cashel

This is another small stone fort (cashel) which was built in the middle of the first millennium AD, about 1,500 years after the hillfort.

This cashel was built with stone taken from the ramparts of the hillfort and was occupied by a single or extended family who farmed the area around the hill (Fig. 23 and Information Panel 4). The foundations of a small house are preserved against the inner northern side. This site has an unusual outer defensive stone bank visible about 20 metres to the north and west of the main cashel wall. Some of the field walls on the hill were probably part of the farmland associated with the cashel as are a number of unenclosed houses on the western hill slope below the cashel.

Aerial view of Mooghaun hillfort from the east showing the upper and lower cashels. (Michael Herity).

Fig. 23
Reconstruction drawing of the second early historic cashel. (David Hill).

Acknowledgements

The North Munster Project spent over five years in the field in the Mooghaun area and made many valuable friends who contributed enormously, not only to the research but also to the enjoyment of our time in Clare. We owe a particular debt to our most gracious hostess, Deirdre O'Brien-Vaughan, who provided a haven of friendship, wit, music and fun (but also very many late nights ☺). Mrs Mona Clancy offered many particular kindnesses. The considerable interest of John Higgins, John O'Brien, and Hugh Tuohy, was of enormous benefit as was the support of the Shannon Archaeological Society and in particular its editors during the period, Catherine O'Donovan and Sonia Schorman. Throughout the research the late Tom Coffey was a stalwart friend and advisor who is much missed.

Over the years, over two hundred people from Ireland, Britain, Spain, France, Germany, Switzerland, Canada, the United States of America and Serbia, professional archaeologists, students and interested amateurs, worked on the Project in the area: to all of them our thanks for the dedicated work and the good company. I would particularly like to mention some local people who made a special contribution – John Murphy, Frank Daly, Fiona Reilly, and Caoilfhionn Vaughan. My thanks to Coillte Teo., the owners of Mooghaun during the excavation, for their generous permission to work on the site.

The support of the Directorate of the Discovery Programme is warmly acknowledged, and very particularly the support and assistance of the Programme Manager, Brian Lacey, and Jennifer Cunningham whose considerable help has made this volume possible. The reconstruction drawings of David Hill provide a handsome illumination of the past. The professionalism and imagination of Metaphor, and especially that of Michael Lynch, has added considerably to the success of this venture. My very special thanks to my colleagues on the Project staff, Tom Condit, Finola O'Carroll, Aidan O'Sullivan, Aoife Daly and Ines Hagen, and to the Data Manager of the Discovery Programme, Barry Masterson. Helen Roche, Aidan O'Sullivan, Ann Lynch and Jack Harrison very kindly read drafts of the text and made many helpful suggestions.

Mooghaun hillfort was taken into state ownership in 1996 by Dúchas, The Heritage Service of the Department of Arts, Heritage, Gaeltacht and the Islands. My thanks to them for all their on-going co-operation. The on-site information panels produced by Dúchas, which provide the basis for part of this book, were a co-operative venture between Eoin Grogan, Jack Harrison and David Hill (John Harrison and Associates), and Ann Lynch and Terry Dunne (Dúchas). Finally, my thanks to The National Museum of Ireland (Figs 4, 5 and 8), Professor Michael Herity (page 44), and Aoife Daly (pages 31, 33 and 41) for their photographs, and to The National Museum of Wales for the reconstruction of a votive offering (Fig. 3).

Suggested reading

General background

Cooney, G. and Grogan, E. 1994 *Irish Prehistory, a social perspective*. Wordwell, Dublin.

Harbison, P. 1988 *Pre-Christian Ireland*, Thames and Hudson. London.

Herity, M. and Eogan, G. 1977 *Ireland in Prehistory*. Routledge and Kegan Paul, London.

Mitchell, F. and Ryan, M. 1997 *Reading the Irish Landscape*. Town House, Dublin.

O'Kelly, M. J. 1989 *Early Ireland*. Cambridge University Press, Cambridge.

Raftery, B. 1994 *Pagan Celtic Ireland. The Enigma of the Irish Iron Age*. Thames and Hudson, London.

Waddell, J. 1998 *The Prehistoric Archaeology of Ireland*. Galway University Press, Galway.

Mooghaun and the prehistory of south-east Clare

Bennett, I. and Grogan, E. 1993a Excavations at Mooghaun South, Co. Clare.
   Preliminary report on the 1992 season, *Discovery Programme Reports* **1**, 39-43, Dublin.

Condit, T. 1995 Hillfort discoveries near Killaloe, Co. Clare, *Archaeology Ireland* **31**, 34-37.

Condit, T. 1996 Gold and *fulachta fiadh* - the Mooghaun find, 1854, *Archaeology Ireland* **38**, 20-23.

Condit, T. and O'Sullivan, A. 1996 Fermoyle hillfort and later prehistoric landscapes in east Clare,
   The Other Clare **20**, 39-45.

Condit, T., Synnott, P. and Masterson, B. 1994 Planning the Prehistoric Past, *Archaeology Ireland* **30**, 20-23.

Grogan, E. 1995 Excavations at Mooghaun South, 1993, Interim report,
   Discovery Programme Reports **2**, 57-61, Dublin.

Grogan, E. 1996a Excavations at Mooghaun South, 1994, Interim report,
   Discovery Programme Reports **4**, 47-57, Dublin.

Grogan, E. 1996b Changing Places: settlement patterns in prehistory, *The Other Clare* **20**, 48-52.

Grogan, E. and Condit, T. 1994 The later prehistoric landscape of south-east Clare, *The Other Clare* **18**, 8-12.

Grogan, E., Condit, T., O'Carroll, F. and O'Sullivan, A. 1995
   A preliminary assessment of the prehistoric landscape of the Mooghaun study area,
   Discovery Programme Reports **2**, 47-56, Dublin.

Grogan, E. Condit, T., O'Carroll, F., O'Sullivan, A. and Daly, A. 1996
   Tracing the late prehistoric landscape in North Munster,
   Discovery Programme Reports **4**, 26-46, Dublin.

Grogan, E., O'Carroll, F., Condit, T., O'Sullivan, A. and Daly, A. 1993
   The Prehistoric Dark Age in North Munster, *Archaeology Ireland* **24**, 16-19.

Grogan, E., O'Sullivan, A., O'Carroll, F. and Hagen, I. 1999
   Knocknalappa, Co. Clare: a reappraisal, *Discovery Programme Reports* **5**, Dublin.

O'Carroll, F. 1994 Hoards of the later prehistoric period, *Archaeology Ireland* **28**, 11-13.

O'Carroll, F. 1999 The North Munster Project: the artefact research, *Discovery Programme Monographs*.

O'Carroll, F. and Condit, T. 1993
   Objects and their landscape: the integrated study, *Discovery Programme Reports* **1**, 36-38, Dublin.

O'Carroll, F. and Ryan, M. 1995
   A Late Bronze Age hoard at Enagh East, Co. Clare,
   North Munster Antiquarian Journal **34**, 3-12.

O'Sullivan, A. 1994 Harvesting the waters, *Archaeology Ireland* **27**, 10-12.

O'Sullivan, A. 1995 Marshlanders, *Archaeology Ireland* **31**, 8-11.

O'Sullivan, A. 1996a
   Later Bronze Age discoveries on North Munster estuaries, *Discovery Programme Reports* **4**, 63-71, Dublin.

O'Sullivan, A. 1996b
   An Early Historic Period fishweir on the Fergus Estuary, Co. Clare, *North Munster Antiquarian Journal* **35**, 52-61.

O'Sullivan, A. and Condit, T. 1995
   Late Bronze Age settlement and economy by the marshlands of the upper Fergus estuary, *The Other Clare* **19**, 5-9.

Synnott, P. 1996
   Geographical Information Systems - an archaeological application, *Discovery Programme Reports* **4**, 73-84, Dublin.

Raftery, J. 1942 Knocknalappa crannóg, Co. Clare., *North Munster Antiquarian Journal* **3**, 53-72.

Westropp, T. J. 1908 Types of the Ring-forts and Similar Structures remaining in Eastern Clare
   (The Newmarket Group) *Proceedings of the Royal Irish Academy* **27C**, 217-234.

The final excavation reports, as well as the assessment of the prehistoric archaeology of south-east Clare, are due for publication as a Discovery Programme Monograph in 2000. The *Discovery Programme Reports* are available from the Discovery Programme, 13-15 Lower Hatch Street, Dublin 2 (www.discoveryprogramme.ie), the Royal Irish Academy, Dawson Street, Dublin 2, and selected bookshops. The Shannon Archaeological and Historical Society, Shannon, Co. Clare publish *The Other Clare*. Archaeology Ireland is a popular quarterly magazine (Archaeology Ireland Ltd., P.O. Box 69, Bray, Co. Wicklow) available from large newsagents.